D0460644

Why Do Plants Have Flowers?

And Other Questions About Evolution and Classification

PAT JACOBS

PowerKiDS press

Published in 2017 by
The Rosen Publishing Group, Inc.
29 East 21st Street, New York, NY 10010

Cataloging-in-Publication Data
Names: Jacobs, Pat.
Title: Why do plants have flowers? / Pat Jacobs.
Description: New York : PowerKids Press, 2017. | Series: Wildlife wonders | Includes index.
Identifiers: ISBN 9781508153481 (pbk.) | ISBN 9781499432732 (library bound) | ISBN 9781508153382 (6 pack)
Subjects: LCSH: Plants--Juvenile literature. | Plants--Evolution--Juvenile literature.
Classification: LCC QK49.J33 2017 | DDC 580--d23

Series Editor: Julia Bird
Packaged by: Dynamo Limited

Picture credits
Key: **t**=top, **m**=middle, **b**=bottom, **l**=left, **r**=right
Cover: graph/Shutterstock, Thampapon/Shutterstock, irin-k/Shutterstock, StesŠin Yevgeniy/Shutterstock; p1 graph/Shutterstock, Thampapon/Shutterstock; p3 irin-k/Shutterstock, StesŠin Yevgeniy/Shutterstock; p4 **t** DeLoyd Huenink/Shutterstock, p4 **b** Scisetti Alfio/Shutterstock, LianeM/Shutterstock; p5 **t** MIMOHE/Shutterstock, p5 **b** Kseniia Perminova/Shutterstock; 6 (algae) Nagel Photography/Shutterstock, (liverwort) Giuseppe Lancia/Shutterstock, (cycad) 97584608/Shutterstock; p7 (cactus) 145107019, (bean) Stefanie Mohr Photography/Shutterstock, (lily) Nazzu/Shutterstock, (gardenia) Donjiy/Shutterstock, (rose) Chamille White / Shutterstock, (grass) 128908232/Shutterstock, (maple) Tatiana Grozetskaya/Shutterstock; p8 **t** L_amica/Shutterstock, p8 **bl** Denis and Yulia Pogostins/Shutterstock, p8 **br** Filipe B. Varela/Shutterstock; p9 **t** Mikhail Olykainen/Shutterstock, p9 **b** Archiwiz Snowbelle Potapov Alexander rawcaptured/Shutterstock; p10 **t** Andrea Danti/Shutterstock, p10 **b** Designua/Shutterstock; p11 **t** Dr. Morley Read/Shutterstock, p11 **b** nico99/Shutterstock; p12 **t** BlueRingMedia/Shutterstock, p12 **b** (catkins) Konrad Weiss/Shutterstock, p12 **b** (flower) Imfoto/Shutterstock; p13 **t** Andreas Zerndl/Shutterstock, p13 **b** Arto Hakola/Shutterstock; p14 **t** PRILL/Shutterstock, p14 **b** Diane Garcia/Shutterstock; p15 **t** Aleksey Klints/Shutterstock, p15 **b** Dynamo Limited; p16 **t** Norberto Mario Lauria/Shutterstock, p16 **b** Sally Scott/Shutterstock; p17 **t** vilax/Shutterstock, p17 **m** baitong333/Shutterstock, p17 **b** Richard Griffin/Shutterstock; p18 **t** 9548315445/Shutterstock, p18 **b** Vladimir Melnik/Shutterstock; p19 **t** Patrick Poendl/Shutterstock, p19 **b** Surbucca/ Shutterstock; p20 **t** hwongcc/Shutterstock, p20 **b** Ethan Daniels/Shutterstock; p21 **t** Oleg Znamenskiy/Shutterstock, p21 **b** Paul Vinten/Shutterstock; p22 **t** Le Do/Shutterstock, p22 **b** PHOTO FUN/Shutterstock; p23 **t** Fabio Sacchi/Shutterstock, p23 **b** Andrew Fletcher/Shutterstock; p24 **t** Alexander Petrenko/Shutterstock, p24 **b** Jakkrit Orrasri/Shutterstock; p25 **t** kkaplin/Shutterstock, p25 **b** Joy Stein/Shutterstock; p26 **tr** Egor Rodynchenko/Shutterstock, p26 **tl** Stephen B. Goodwin/Shutterstock, p26 **b** Denis and Yulia Pogostins/Shutterstock; p27 **t** Jiang Hongyan, Kalin Eftimov, Joseph S.L. Tan Matt, Potapov Alexander/Shutterstock, p27 **b** Silhouette Lover/Shutterstock; p28 **t** Leighton Photography & Imaging/Shutterstock, p28 **b** scaners3d/Shutterstock; p29 **t** KAMONRAT/Shutterstock, p29 **b** pedrosala/Shutterstock; p30 **t** Tischenko Irina/Shutterstock, p30 **b** Milosz_M/Shutterstock

Manufactured in the United States of America
CPSIA Compliance Information: Batch #BW17PK: For Further Information contact Rosen Publishing, New York, New York at 1-800-237-9932.

Contents

Words in **bold** can be found in the glossary on page 31.

What is a plant?

Plants are the only living things that can make their own food from sunlight. Without them, life on Earth would not exist. Plants produce oxygen, which made it possible for other forms of life to **evolve**.

The tropical rain forest is home to millions of animals. Its many plants generate much of the world's oxygen.

How plants evolved

The first land plants were mosses that probably evolved from algae (see page 6) growing in water about 500 million years ago. Without water to support them, land plants needed stiff stems so they could grow taller. The ferns and horsetails that appeared about 350 million years ago were among the first plants to develop these strong stems.

Horsetails are among the oldest plants on Earth. Some grew to the size of trees during the Carboniferous period, 359–299 million years ago.

The first forests

The earliest plants were below knee height, but as they developed stronger tissues that could carry water and **nutrients** up longer stems, they were able to grow taller. The earliest known tree is the *Wattieza*, which evolved about 385 million years ago and looked like a tree fern. It was followed by conifers, ginkgoes and cycads (see page 6).

The ginkgo biloba tree has unique, fan-shaped leaves.

Flowers appear

Flowering plants changed the world. They evolved about 150 million years ago and flourished during the Cretaceous period, 144 to 65 million years ago, when dinosaurs ruled the Earth. Almost all the food we eat comes from flowering plants or from animals that feed on them.

*Magnolias were among the first flowering plants to appear on Earth. They were probably **pollinated** by beetles as bees had yet to evolve.*

Classification of plants

The plant kingdom includes more than 400,000 identified **species** and the list is growing all the time. Plants are usually **classified** according to the structure of their stems, leaves and flowers. Flowering plants (shown on page 7) make up the largest group, with more than 300 different families. Some of the most important plant families are listed here.

Algae

Algae produce their own food through photosynthesis (see page 10) but they do not have roots, leaves or stems. They can survive in the harshest habitats, from deserts to the Arctic Circle.

Mosses, liverworts and hornworts

These plants do not flower. They grow from **spores** (see page 17), not seeds. They are small, with simple leaves, and usually live in damp shade.

Ferns, horsetails and club moss

These plants were among the first to grow on land. They reproduce from spores and have stems that carry water and nutrients to the leaves.

Conifers

These trees have waxy, needle-like or scaly leaves. They do not flower. Instead they have male cones that produce pollen. This is blown onto female cones, which then develop seeds.

Cycads

These nonflowering plants have trunks with a crown of stiff, **evergreen** leaves. They grow in warm parts of the world and produce large cones.

Ginkgoes

The *ginkgo biloba* is the only surviving member of this group of trees, which first appeared about 250 million years ago. Male trees produce cones and female trees have fleshy seeds.

Cacti

Most cacti live in very dry environments and have evolved to save water in their enlarged stems. Most have lost their original leaves, and have spines, which are modified leaves.

Daisy family

This huge family of flowering plants includes about 23,000 species. They have **colonized** most parts of the world, from the Arctic to the tropics.

Pea and bean family

This group makes up the third largest family of land plants. Many have **nodules** on their roots that absorb nitrogen from the air to help the plant grow.

Lily family

Lilies grow from **bulbs** or **rhizomes**. They have long, narrow leaves and often have attractive flowers. Many species are poisonous.

Orchid family

Orchids make up one of the largest and most widespread families of plants. They are found on every continent except Antarctica.

Coffee family

This little-known family of plants is the fifth largest. As well as coffee trees, it includes gardenias (right) and cinchona, which gives us a drug called quinine.

Rose family

Apart from roses, this group includes many types of fruit trees and plants, including apples, peaches, almonds, cherries, raspberries and strawberries.

Grass family

Grasses include important crops, such as wheat, rice, corn and oats. Grasses grow from the base of the plant, not the tip, so they can be mown and grazed without suffering damage.

Magnolia family

Magnolias are trees and shrubs that can be evergreen or **deciduous**. They were among the first flowering plants and date back to the Cretaceous period.

Maple family

These trees and shrubs have clusters of small flowers and often have colorful autumn leaves. Sap from the sugar maple is made into maple syrup.

Parts of a plant

When plants moved onto land, they developed roots, stems and leaves. These contain a network of tubes and veins that carry water and nutrients from the soil to every part of the plant.

It is easy to see the veins of this maple leaf. They supply the leaf with water and minerals that have traveled up the tree from its roots.

Roots

Roots keep a plant anchored into the ground and suck up water and minerals. Some plants, such as carrots, have a long, thick taproot, while others have a mass of fibrous roots. Plant roots are important for holding light soils together and stopping them from being **eroded**.

Taproots (far left) have tiny hairlike roots sprouting from them. A plant with fibrous roots (near left) has a lot of thin roots branching from the stem.

Stems and trunks

A plant's stem supports the plant and helps it to reach up towards the Sun. Stems are packed with tiny tubes that carry water and nutrients to the leaves. Tree trunks are in essence giant stems that are covered by a protective layer of bark. Water and nutrients (the sap) are carried by the soft, outer layers of sapwood, just underneath the bark, while the hard heartwood in the center supports the tree.

A tree grows a new ring of cells beneath its bark each year, so you can find the age of the tree by counting its rings.

Evergreen leaves, such as the ivy leaf on the left, remain on the plant for up to 20 years.

Leaves

Leaves are made up of layers of cells that make food for the plant, sandwiched between a tough, waxy coating that protects the leaf and stops it drying out. In autumn, deciduous plants stop producing green **chlorophyll** (see page 10). Their leaves change color, then they fall off. Evergreen plants keep their leaves throughout the year.

Leaves come in many different shapes.

Cactus spines (below) are modified leaves.

Fern leaves (above) are called fronds.

Some plants have compound leaves (above), which are divided into separate leaflets.

The leaves of deciduous plants, such as the oak leaf above, change color before they drop.

9

A light diet

Like all living things, plants need food to survive. The difference is that plants produce their own food from sunlight, carbon dioxide and water using a process called photosynthesis.

A plant needs sunlight, carbon dioxide, water and nutrients.

Sunlight is absorbed by the chlorophyll in the leaves.

Oxygen produced during photosynthesis is released into the air.

The leaves absorb a gas called carbon dioxide from the air.

The roots take up water and nutrients from the soil.

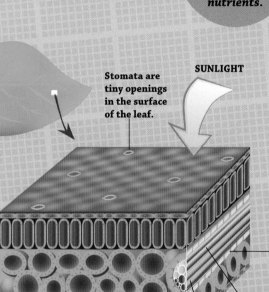

SUNLIGHT

Stomata are tiny openings in the surface of the leaf.

Veins contain tissues called xylem and phloem.

Xylem transports water and minerals around the plant.

Phloem carries the sugars that are made during photosynthesis to every cell in the plant.

OXYGEN   **CARBON DIOXIDE**

Plants breathe out oxygen and breathe in carbon dioxide through the stomata in their leaves.

How photosynthesis works

Leaves are a plant's powerhouse. They contain chlorophyll, a green substance that absorbs sunlight. This provides the plant with the energy to turn carbon dioxide and water into sugar, which feeds the plant, and oxygen, which the plant breathes out. Photosynthesis first developed in **bacteria** that lived at least 2.8 billion years ago.

Freeloaders

Some plants steal the food they need from others and may eventually kill their host. These **parasites** do not need green leaves because they do not make any of their own food through photosynthesis. **Hemiparasites**, such as mistletoe, take water and minerals from trees, but have green leaves because they still produce their own food.

Dodder is a parasite that coils its orange stems around its host, while rootlike growths steal water and food from the host's stem.

Meat-eating plants

Some plants that grow in poor soils get nutrients by luring insects into deadly traps, where they are dissolved by the plant's digestive juices. They include sundews that capture victims with sticky hairs and pitcher plants, which drown insects inside their slippery-sided traps. The Venus flytrap's leaves snap shut to imprison their prey when sensitive hairs on their surface are triggered.

It takes about ten days for a Venus flytrap to digest its prey.

Why do plants have flowers?

Plants have flowers to reproduce (make new plants). Most flowers contain the male and female parts of a plant. These are surrounded by petals, which attract pollinating insects. The male parts, called stamens, produce **pollen**. When pollen lands on the female part called the stigma, **fertilization** occurs and seeds are produced.

Stigma

Style

Anther

Ovary – this contains the ova (eggs). When fertilized, each becomes a seed.

Petal

Filament

The female part of a flower (the pistil) consists of the stigma, style and ovary. The male part (the stamen) is made up of the filament and the anther.

Pollination

Some plants, including sunflowers, can pollinate themselves, but most need pollen from another plant of the same species. Some plants rely on insects or other animals to transfer pollen from plant to plant, while others have light pollen that is blown by the wind.

Hazel trees have male catkins (right) which produce pollen. The pollen is blown onto the female flowers (above), by the wind.

Attracting a pollinator

Plants that need to attract pollinators are often sweetly scented with brightly colored petals. Most contain a sugary liquid called nectar, so visitors get a sweet drink in exchange for transferring their pollen.

Bee orchids look and smell like a female bee to attract males. The male bees then carry pollen to another orchid.

Unusual pollinators

Insects, birds and bats make good pollinators because they can fly from flower to flower, but some plants rely on other animals to do the job. These include galagos, sugar gliders, lizards and slugs. The Madagascan traveler's palm is thought to have evolved at the same time as the ruffed lemur (right), which is its main pollinator.

Black and white ruffed lemurs use their strong fingers to open the tough, spiky leaves that protect the flowers of the traveler's palm tree to reach the nectar inside.

Setting seed

When plants started to grow on land, they needed a way to spread. The evolution of seeds meant that the **embryos** of plants were protected inside a tough shell and could travel far and wide.

Dandelion flowers use the wind to spread their seeds over a wide area where they have space to grow.

How seeds are spread

Plants cannot move so they rely on animals, wind, water and exploding seedpods to colonize new environments. Some seeds, such as dandelion and thistle seeds, have their own parachutes so the slightest breeze will lift them high in the sky. Others have little hooks that stick to the fur of passing animals. Himalayan balsam seedpods explode when they are touched, shooting the seeds up to 23 feet (7 m) away.

Some seeds have prickly seed cases that cling to animals' fur or people's clothes.

Fruit and nuts

Some seeds are surrounded by juicy fruits. They attract animals that eat the fruits and often carry the seeds away from the parent plant. Then the animals spit out the seeds, or get rid of them in their droppings, and the seed is able to grow into a new plant. Nuts are seeds with hard shells. Animals often bury these to eat during the winter months.

Squirrels bury nuts to eat in winter. Some are never found, and grow into new trees.

The life cycle of a plant

When a seed lands in the right spot, it germinates (starts to grow) and a new plant is born.

1 **A seed germinates and roots begin to form under the soil.**

2 **The seedling emerges from the ground.**

3 **The plant gets taller and more leaves grow.**

4 **The flower buds open and insects carry pollen from one flower to another.**

5 **The fertilized flowers form seedpods.**

6 **The seeds fall to the ground and some grow into new plants.**

1   2   3   4   5   6

Spreading without seeds

Some plants can spread through asexual reproduction, which means they need only one parent. Young plants that are produced in this way are identical to each other and to the parent.

An easy way to make a new plant through asexual reproduction is to cut off a nonflowering shoot and leave it in water or moist soil until it grows roots.

Bulbs and corms

Bulbs and **corms** are thick underground stems that are swollen with food. They often reproduce by sprouting extra bulbs or corms next to the parent. Onions, daffodils and tulips grow from bulbs and crocuses grow from corms.

Some plants can reproduce both asexually and from seed. For example, daffodils form new bulbs that separate from the parent, as seen here, and also produce seeds.

Creeping stems

Some plants, such as buttercups and strawberries, grow creeping stems called stolons that spread along the ground. When the stem reaches a certain length, it forms a new plant. Once the young plant is established, the stolon withers away.

Strawberry plants produce long stolons called runners. The young plants can be moved to make a new strawberry bed.

Tubers and rhizomes

Tubers and rhizomes are both types of stem. Rhizomes spread horizontally along the surface or underground, and produce new shoots. Tubers are swollen stems, which include potatoes and yams. They multiply underground and store food ready to produce a new plant in spring.

Ginger root is actually a rhizome (see right), which is a type of stem.

Borne on the wind

Mosses, horsetails, and ferns – some of the first plants to grow on land – do not produce flowers or seeds. Instead they make spores, which are dustlike particles that are blown away by the wind. They can travel long distances and have been found at heights above 32,800 feet (10,000 m).

The leaf of a small fern may shed 750,000 spores.

Harsh habitats

By adapting their roots, leaves, stems or size, plants have evolved to grow almost everywhere in the world – from snowy mountainsides to muddy marshes and from arid deserts to the Arctic **tundra**.

Conifers have adapted to grow in cold climates. Their leaves are protected by a thick, waxy coating and the trees are a conical shape so that snow slides off their branches.

The Arctic poppy has dish-shaped flowers that follow the Sun. They need to absorb as much heat as possible to produce seeds before winter returns.

Tundra

The tundra is cold all year round and the soil beneath the surface is permanently frozen. Plants that live there have shallow roots and grow close to the ground. They have dark leaves that absorb the Sun's heat during the short Arctic summer. Some plants have hairy leaves and most grow in clumps to keep warm.

Mountains

Cold, windswept mountains present particular problems for plants. They have adapted by staying small and growing in thick cushions or flat mats that hug the ground to keep out of the harsh winds. Plants that grow on mountaintops in tropical regions have to endure strong sunlight, so they often have leaves covered in fine hairs that provide a built-in sunscreen.

Mountain plants grow close to the ground to avoid being damaged by the wind.

Deserts

Desert plants have to cope with scorching days, cold nights and little rain. Some plants, called succulents, have adapted to survive for years between rainstorms by storing water in their thick stems or leaves. Many also have waxy coatings or hair to reduce water loss. Their long roots spread out widely to collect as much water as possible when rain falls.

Succulents are a tempting source of food and water for desert animals so cacti, such as these, have evolved sharp spines to avoid being eaten.

19

Water plants

Today's aquatic flowering plants have evolved from plants that once lived on land, and then returned to the water. Plants that have adapted to live in water range from microscopic algae to giant water lilies.

The water hyacinth is one of the world's fastest-growing plants. It spreads by both seeds and stolons.

Algae and seaweeds

Algae are simple plants that do not have stems, leaves or flowers, although they contain chlorophyll and make their own food. Seaweeds are a type of algae. They have fronds that are similar to leaves and some have bubble-like air bladders to keep them afloat. Instead of roots, they have **holdfasts** that attach to solid objects.

Some types of algae are so small that they can be seen only through a microscope, but this seaweed, called giant kelp, grows up to 146 feet (45 m) long.

Floating plants

Plants such as the water lily float on the surface of the water and are anchored to the bottom by their roots. They have flexible stems that move with the water's current. Chlorophyll is found only in the leaf surface that is exposed to the Sun, so the reverse side of a water lily leaf is a reddish color, while the top is green.

Water lilies have large, waxy leaves that spread across the surface of the water to make the most of the sunlight.

Pencil-like aerial roots grow vertically from a mangrove tree's underwater root system to provide the tree with oxygen.

Wetland trees

Most plants cannot survive in waterlogged soil, but the roots of trees that grow in wetlands are often completely covered by water. Mangroves have overcome this problem by evolving special structures that stick up out of the water and act like snorkels to provide oxygen for their roots.

Self-defense

Plants cannot escape from their predators, so they have evolved other ways to keep their enemies at bay. Many plants are armed with thorns and spines to stop hungry animals from getting too close.

Grazing animals avoid thistles because they have spines on their stems, leaves and even their flower buds.

Chemical warfare

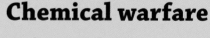

The hairs on the leaves of stinging nettles are like tiny needles that inject painful chemicals into the skin of anyone who brushes against them. Other plants that cause a painful rash include poison ivy, poison oak and poison sumac. All parts of the machineel tree cause painful skin blisters – even a drop of rain trickling down the tree is dangerous.

Stinging nettles support more than 40 species of insect. They move between the hairs without activating the sting.

Ant army

Some species of acacia tree protect their juicy leaves from insects and animals by offering a home to an army of ants. The ants drink the sweet nectar produced at the base of the tree's leaves and, in exchange, they attack any creatures, from crickets to goats, that threaten the tree. They even destroy seedlings growing at the tree's base that might take its nutrients and block out sunlight.

The acacia trees produce chemicals in their flowers that ants do not like. Ant guards, such as this one, stay away from the flowers, so pollinating insects are safe from attack.

Deadly poison

Many plants are poisonous, including some you might find in your garden, such as oleander, laburnum, monkshood and the castor oil plant. The seeds of the castor oil plant can be used to produce ricin, a poison that is deadly if it is inhaled or injected. Some animals are specially adapted to cope with the toxins in certain plants. Cinnabar moth caterpillars feed on poisonous ragwort, which, in turn, makes them poisonous to predators.

Cinnabar moth caterpillars have yellow and black stripes to warn predators that they are poisonous.

Record-breaking plants

Plants vary in size from microscopic waterweeds to towering trees. The tallest trees are the giant redwoods found in California, which reach a height of 377 feet (115 m).

The giant redwood's bark can be 35 feet (9 m) thick at the base, which protects the tree from forest fires.

Smallest flowering plant

The smallest flowering plant is a duckweed called watermeal. It is less than 0.08 inch (2 mm) long and weighs about the same as two grains of salt. Its flower has no petals and is almost impossible to see because it just looks like a dent in the center of the tiny plant.

Watermeal plants are half the size of a grain of rice.

Largest flower

The *Rafflesia arnoldii* flower measures about 3.3 feet (1 m) across, making it the largest individual flower on Earth. It is nicknamed the "corpse flower" because it stinks of rotting meat. The foul smell attracts flies and beetles, which pollinate the plant.

Rafflesia arnoldii *grows in the rain forests of Southeast Asia.*

Ancient trees

A spruce tree discovered in Sweden is growing from a cluster of roots that are 9,550 years old, and the root system of a colony of 47,000 quaking aspen trees growing in Utah is thought to be 80,000 years old. The oldest single living tree is a Great Basin bristlecone pine, which stands in the White Mountains in California. It is more than 5,000 years old.

Great Basin bristlecone pines grow very slowly. They are among the oldest living organisms in the world.

Artificial selection

Many of the plants we see around us are not wholly the work of nature. Over the centuries, humans have interfered in the natural evolution of plants by breeding varieties that produce larger crops, have better flowers or are resistant to disease.

Plant breeders have adapted the wild daffodil (top) to create new varieties, such as this white daffodil with double petals.

This plant breeder is fertilizing female marrow flowers using a paintbrush covered in pollen from a carefully selected male flower.

Selective breeding

In nature, most plants are perennials. They grow from the same roots year after year. However, most of the plants that we cultivate are annuals, which survive for just one growing season, because they produce bigger crops. This gives plant breeders a chance to improve varieties each year by choosing the best parents and fertilizing the flowers by hand.

Broccoli

Kale

Wild mustard

Kohlrabi

A variety of vegetables

Broccoli, cauliflower, cabbage, kale and kohlrabi were all created by plant breeders from the wild mustard plant. Broccoli and cauliflower have been modified from the mustard's yellow blooms, kale and cabbage are enlarged mustard leaves and kohlrabi is its swollen stem.

These plants have all been developed from wild mustard. Other brassicas include turnips (swollen roots) and Brussel sprouts (buds).

The plant hunters

A typical garden contains a number of plants that would not naturally be found where the garden is located. Many plants that we think of as **natives** were brought here from other continents by plant hunters who traveled around the world in search of new species.

Potatoes and tomatoes, which are related, were unknown in Europe until explorers brought them back from Latin America in the 16th century.

A green future?

The climate on Earth has been changing ever since plants first evolved. During this time, species either adapted to suit the new conditions, spread to more suitable locations or became **extinct**. Now, plants have to face both **climate change** and loss of habitat caused by humans.

The Cayman Islands ghost orchid is at risk of extinction because its forest habitat is being destroyed.

Seed survival

Plants cannot move when the climate changes or a disaster such as a flood or fire occurs, but they have a survival strategy that other living things do not. Because plants produce seeds that survive for many years, they can grow again when conditions are right. Now, thousands of seed banks have been set up around the world to store seeds in case a species of plant is wiped out.

Scientists in Russia have recently grown plants from Silene seeds stored away in permafrost by squirrels 30,000 years ago.

As the world's population increases, scientists are looking for new ways to grow enough food to feed us all. One solution, where land is scarce, could be to grow food crops indoors using high-intensity lights that mimic sunlight. Instead of being rooted in soil, plants would grow **hydroponically**, in water mixed with nutrients.

Hydroponic crops save water because it can be reused instead of sinking into the soil. They are easier to harvest and suffer from fewer pests and diseases.

Genetically modified plants

By making changes to a plant's **genes**, scientists can produce crops that are resistant to pests and need less land, water and fertilizer. As well as increasing the harvest, genetic modification can add extra vitamins to plants to make them more nutritious. Some people feel that it is dangerous to alter plants' genes. Others believe it is a way to feed the world.

Scientists transfer genes from one plant to another in a laboratory to produce new varieties that have particular qualities, such as resistance to disease.

Incredible plants

Plants are vital to life on Earth. Here are just a few of the many amazing facts about the world's huge variety of vegetation, without which we could not exist.

Seeds on display
A strawberry has about 200 seeds and it is the only fruit that has its seeds on the outside.

Insect guides
Many flowers have ultraviolet patterns on their petals, which insects can see, but we cannot. The patterns guide the insects towards the flower's nectar.

Tree of life
An average tree produces enough oxygen in one year to keep a family of four breathing.

Long-distance traveler
The seed of a plant called Mary's bean drifted more than 15,000 miles (24,000 km) across the ocean from the Marshall Islands in the north Pacific to the coast of Norway.

Exploding seedpod
The Caribbean sandbox tree has a large, pumpkin-shaped seedpod that explodes like a grenade, scattering its seeds and pieces of shell up to 46 feet (14 m) away.

Huge cactus
The giant saguaro cactus can reach 66 feet (20 m) in height and weigh 6.6 tons (6 mt).

Fast growers
Some types of bamboo can grow almost 3.3 feet (1 m) in just one day.

Longest taproot
The mesquite tree, which grows in the desert, has the longest taproot of any plant. It can reach 190 feet (58 m) below the ground.

Tiny tree
A dwarf willow tree that grows in the Arctic tundra is just 2.4 inches (6 cm) tall.

Giant seeds
The coco-de-mer palm, found in the Seychelles, produces seeds (below) that weigh up to 40 pounds (18 kg).

Glossary

Bacteria Tiny life forms. Some cause disease (we call these germs) and others are useful.

Bulb A swollen underground plant stem that stores water and nutrients and has layers, such as an onion

Chlorophyll A green substance, present in all green plants, that absorbs light to provide energy for photosynthesis

Classified Organized into groups

Climate change A change in the weather, often thought to be caused by human activity

Colonize To establish itself in a particular area

Corm A swollen underground plant stem that stores water and nutrients and is solid, unlike a bulb, which is made up of layers

Deciduous Trees and shrubs that lose their leaves for part of the year, either in winter or during the dry season

Embryo The part of a seed that grows into a plant

Erode To gradually wear away, usually as a result of wind or water

Evergreen Trees and shrubs that keep their leaves all through the year

Evolve To develop gradually over generations

Extinct A species with no living members

Fertilization The process that happens when the pollen and the ovule (part of the ovary) join together to make a seed

Genes Sections of DNA (a list of instructions that tells cells what to do) that are passed on from parent to offspring

Hemiparasite A plant that may get part of its food from another, but also creates its own food through photosynthesis

Holdfast A rootlike structure that anchors plants that grow in water to the ground

Hydroponic A method of growing plants in water with added nutrients, instead of in soil

Native A plant or animal that originally lived in a particular place

Nodule A small swelling (on a plant's roots)

Nutrients The food a plant needs to grow

Parasite A plant that lives and feeds on another and does not produce its own food

Pollen A fine, powdery substance released by the male part of a flower, which fertilizes the female part so it can produce seeds

Pollinate To carry pollen to a flower

Rhizome An underground stem that grows roots and shoots

Species A group of wildlife that has similar features and can breed with one another

Spores Tiny dustlike particles produced by some nonflowering plants that can grow into new plants

Tundra A huge, flat part of Europe, Asia and North America that lies within the Arctic region, where the soil beneath the surface is permanently frozen

Index

Websites

PowerKids Press has developed an online list of websites related to the subject of this book. This site is updated regularly. Please use this link to access the list:

www.powerkidslinks.com/ww/plants